XAMonline, Inc.
25 First Street, Suite 106
Cambridge, MA 02141
Toll Free: 1-800-509-4128
Email: info@xamonline.com
Web: www.xamonline.com
Fax: 1-617-583-5552

Library of Congress Cataloging-in-Publication Data

Wynne, Sharon A.
   MTEL Communications and Literacy Skills 01 Practice Test 1: Teacher Certification /
   Sharon A. Wynne. -1st ed.
   ISBN: 978-1-60787-207-8
   1. MTEL Communications and Literacy Skills 01 Practice Test 1
   2. Study Guides   3. MTEL   4. Teachers' Certification & Licensure
   5. Careers

Disclaimer:
The opinions expressed in this publication are the sole works of XAMonline and were created independently from the National Education Association, Educational Testing Service, or any State Department of Education, National Evaluation Systems or other testing affiliates.

Between the time of publication and printing, state specific standards as well as testing formats and website information may change that is not included in part or in whole within this product. Sample test questions are developed by XAMonline and reflect similar content as on real tests; however, they are not former tests. XAMonline assembles content that aligns with state standards but makes no claims nor guarantees teacher candidates a passing score. Numerical scores are determined by testing companies such as NES or ETS and then are compared with individual state standards. A passing score varies from state to state.

Printed in the United States of America   œ-1
MTEL Communications and Literacy Skills 01 Practice Test 1
ISBN: 978-1-60787-207-8

COMMUNICATION AND LITERACY SKILLS PRE TEST

Reading Pre Test

DIRECTIONS: *Read the following passages and answer the questions that follow.*

Marching band music began with organized armies. It was necessary for troops to move in a synchronized fashion. Before musical instruments were introduced, a leader would chant or use drum beats to keep the men organized. Music was added to keep the soldiers in good spirits. During the Revolutionary War, soldiers marched to tunes played by fifes and drums. Later, during the Civil War, soldiers marched to bugle corps and drums. During World War I, soldiers marched to bands that played brass and wood wind instruments as well as the drums. The music played during World War I was more elaborate and more enjoyable to listen to than that of music played during other wars. Marching band music also played an important role in the development of jazz.

1. **What does the word "synchronized" mean in the passage?**

   A. Robotic
   B. Organized*
   C. Musical
   D. Revolutionary

2. **What is the main idea of the passage?**

   A. The music played changed in different wars.
   B. Soldiers marched to music in order to keep their spirits uplifted.
   C. Marching band music originated with organized armies. *
   D. Jazz became important because of marching band music.

3. **What is the author's opinion about marching band music?**

   A. The author likes marching band music.
   B. The author doesn't believe music is a necessary part of war.
   C. The author does not understand the connection between music and war.
   D. The author believes that the music of World War I was the best music. *

4. **Why did the author include the last sentence in the passage, "Marching band music also played an important role in the development of jazz"?**

   A. The author is connecting the history of marching band music to the history of jazz. *
   B. The author wants to expose the reader to different types of music.
   C. The author wants to connect marching band music, jazz, and past wars to the history of music.
   D. The author believes that all music is connected to the origination of jazz.

5. **Why did music replace the chanting of early soldiers?**

   A. Music was easier for the soldiers to hear than chanting.
   B. Music kept the soldiers more synchronized with each other.
   C. Music improved the soldier's moods and attitudes. *
   D. Music allowed the soldiers to march faster.

6. **Which is a fact presented in this passage?**

   A. Soldiers preferred the marching band music over the chanting of other soldiers.
   B. The music of World War I was more developed than the music heard during other wars.
   C. During the Civil War soldiers marched to bugles and drums. *
   D. Marching band music is the most important aspect of jazz music.

7. **What type of organizational pattern did the author use in this passage?**

   A. Classification *
   B. Compare-and-contrast
   C. Cause-and-effect
   D. Narrative

Dance Liners Studio is offering special opportunities to current dance member's families and to new families. If a new dancer is referred to the studio, the family that made the referral will receive $25 off of their October tuition fee. Another incentive that is being offered is a "Change of Studio". If someone has already registered their dancer at another dance <u>locale</u> and paid a non-refundable registration fee, they may register at *Dance Liners* instead and the amount already paid will be deducted from their registration fee. A family must simply show a copy of the check they wrote to the other studio. The next registration date will be August 16 – 20. Your help is greatly appreciated in growing our successful dance program and school.

8. **What is another word that could be substituted for the word *locale* in the passage?**

   A.   class
   B.   school*
   C.   local
   D.   avenue

9. **What is the main idea of the passage?**

   A. Special incentives are being offered to increase enrollment at *Dance Liners.**
   B. A "Change of Studio" incentive is being offered by *Dance Liners.*
   C. Current families of *Dance Liners* will be offered a $25 reduction in tuition.
   D. The next registration dates are August 16 – 20.

10. **What is the author's purpose in writing this piece?**

   A. To inform new families of the next registration dates for *Dance Liners Studio.*
   B. To persuade current families to recruit new families to *Dance Liners.**
   C. To inform current families of specials being offered by the studio.
   D. To persuade new families to try a dance class at *Dance Liners Studio.*

11. **Who is the intended audience for this passage?**

   A. Current students of *Dance Liners Studio.*
   B. Those who plan to register for dance classes between August 16 – 20.
   C. Families who are currently enrolled at *Dance Liners* who may know other interested dancers. *
   D. Dancers who are already enrolled in another dance studio.

12. What conclusion can be drawn from this passage?

A. *Dance Liners Studio* is empathetic to tough economic times and is trying to help families save some money.
B. *Dance Liners Studio* has added classes to their fall lineup.
C. More dance studios were started and they are all competing for the same business.
D. Enrollment is down for upcoming classes at *Dance Liners*. *

13. What would be the best graphic representation to accompany this passage?

A. A pictograph that shows the number of dancers in each class.
B. A line graph that shows enrollment for each year since the studio opened.
C. A table that shows the classes offered and the times. *
D. A bar graph that shows the various fees for each class.

I believe that history does indeed repeat itself. Currently the post office is looking for ways to be more efficient, and save money in the process. They have raised the prices of stamps continually since 1885. In 1885 the price of a stamp was $ .02. Today, it costs $ .44 to mail a letter and rates are expected to increase again in 2011. Another venue that the postal service is exploring in order to reduce costs is to reduce the number of delivery days from 6 to 5 forgoing Saturday delivery. The problems the postal service is experiencing have, in part, been blamed on the Internet and the increased usage of email, fax machines, and cellular phones.

The problems that the postal service is facing are not new ideas however. The Pony Express, a special mail service that existed in 1860, was much faster than regular mail. In order for a piece of mail to be delivered from Missouri to California, it took the regular mail approximately three weeks. The Pony Express was able to deliver the same letter in 10 days. However, the Pony Express only lasted about 18 months. In 1861 the telegraph was invented and messages could be sent by wire to California much faster than the Pony Express.

I don't think that the United States Postal Service will cease to exist anytime soon. However, history is often a great measure of what is to come in the future.

14. **What does the word efficient mean in the first paragraph?**

   A. systematic*
   B. quick
   C. thrifty
   D. effective

15. **What is the implied main idea of this passage?**

   A. The postal service today is better off than the Pony Express of the 1800s.
   B. History can be used as a predictor of what will become of the United States Postal Service.*
   C. Technology is the only factor responsible for the decline of the postal service.
   D. The Pony Express was destined to fail based on historical information.

16. **Which group of people would MOST LIKELY not respond favorably to this passage?**

   A. Postal workers *
   B. History teachers
   C. Information Technology specialists
   D. The US Government

17. **What is being compared in this passage?**

   A. The price of stamps
   B. The problems facing the postal service.*
   C. Technology of today and yesterday.
   D. The speed of the Pony Express and regular mail.

18. What argument does the author offer to support the idea that the US Postal Service is declining?

   A. The price of stamps has increased steadily since 1885.
   B. Increased dependence on technology.
   C. Lack of efficiency and continued economic decline.
   D. Historical information about the postal service in the past.
      *

19. Which would be the best diagram to show the change in price of postage stamps over time?

   A. A pie chart
   B. A bar graph
   C. A pictograph
   D. A stem and leaf chart

In 1966 Miranda rights were decided upon and put into law. Miranda required all police officers to notify suspects that were taken into custody that they had the right to remain silent and have a lawyer represent them, even if they were unable to afford one. However, the law has now become a little <u>muddled</u>. Although law officials are still required to read suspects their Miranda rights one big change that has taken affect is that suspects must now verbally notify police officials that they would like to <u>invoke</u> their "right to remain silent". In other words, they must break their silence. In addition, suspects must also tell police that they want a lawyer present during their questioning. Unbelievably, if suspects actually "remain silent" in essence what they are doing is waiving their rights to have an attorney present when they truly choose to remain silent. So, although those who are read their Miranda rights are told that they "have the right to remain silent", they truly don't even have this right any more.

20. What does the author use the word *muddled* in the passage to mean?

    A. complicated
    B. unclear*
    C. shorter
    D. different

21. Which detail supports the idea that the Miranda law has changed?

    A. Suspects must tell police officers that they do not want to say anything. *
    B. Suspects must remain silent if they wish to have their Miranda rights upheld.
    C. Officers must read anyone taken into custody their Miranda rights.
    D. It is not necessary to tell police that they want a lawyer – one will be appointed to them automatically.

22. Why did the author use the word *unbelievably* in the following sentence from the passage?

"Unbelievably, if suspects actually "remain silent" in essence what they are doing is waiving their rights to have an attorney present…"

    A. The author agrees with this change in the law.
    B. The author is showing that this idea is not factual.
    C. The author thinks the idea stated in the sentence is ridiculous.*
    D. The author believes that suspects should not be allowed a lawyer.

23. What does the word *invoke* mean in the passage?

A. apply*
B. pass up
C. be notified
D. pay for

24. Does the author show any evidence of bias in this passage?

A. Yes*
B. No

25. What is the BEST summary for the above passage?

A. Miranda rights have been in effect since 1966.
B. Miranda requires all police officials to notify suspects of their rights upon being taken into custody.
C. Suspects have the right to remain silent but only if they alert officials of their desire to do so.
D. There have been some changes made to the Miranda law which was put into place in 1966. *

The environment and its future have been a top concern of citizens and politicians around the globe. Environmentalists, engineers, and high-ranking officials have been brainstorming ways to continue to grow economies without harming the environment. China is one country that has proven dedicated to this cause and is developing a three-dimensional fast bus. The concept is so interesting in that the bus will "straddle" cars as it carries passengers above. Therefore, no new roadways need to be built or changed since simple tracks are all that the bus needs to follow and these can be installed along the sides of existing roadways. The new speed bus will run on a combination of electricity and solar power and will be able to move up to 60 kilometers per hour as well as carry between 1,200 and 1,600 people. Chinese engineers are not straddling the fence on this new innovative idea; the first tracks are scheduled to be installed toward the conclusion of 2010.

26. **Why does the author say that, "Chinese engineers are not straddling the fence on this new innovative idea..."?**

A. The Chinese are known to move slowly on new and innovative ideas.
B. There are still logistical ideas to be figured out before the project can move forward.
C. The author used the figure of speech to show that the Chinese are moving quickly on their new "straddling" bus idea. *
D. The author wants to show that this is not an old fashioned idea by using this figure of speech.

27. **How does the author support the idea that the new fast bus is interesting?**

A. The bus will straddle cars as it carries passengers above. *
B. No new roadways need to be built or changed.
C. The new fast bus follows tracks that run alongside preexisting roadways.
D. The bus will be able to move up to 60 kilometers per hour.

28. **Who would MOST LIKELY be the most interested in reading this article?**

A. Chinese government officials.
B. United States engineers.
C. Anyone traveling to China near the end of 2010.
D. Environmentally conscious citizens. *

29. **What conclusion can be drawn about the Chinese from this passage?**

A. The Chinese are a very competitive nation.
B. The Chinese can be classified as an innovative nation. *
C. The fast bus project will be completed very quickly.
D. No one is interested in riding the fast bus over driving their cars.

30. **The author states that the environment has been a top concern to those around the globe. Which idea BEST supports this idea?**

A. Chinese engineers are not straddling the fence on implementing the fast bus.
B. Environmentalists, engineers and high-ranking officials have been brainstorming ways to continue to grow economies while preserving the environment.
C. China is developing the fast bus and will begin production as early as 2010. *
D. The new speed bus will run on a combination of electricity and solar power.

CO₂ Generated By Travel Mode

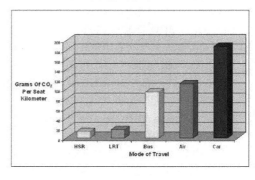

31. **Which conclusion can be drawn from the graph above?**

A. The new fast bus will emit the same amount of CO2 as a car.
B. It is better to fly than to take a bus to a location in order to reduce the amount of CO2 being emitted into the air.
C. The new fast bus will reduce the amount of CO2 emissions.*
D. The fast bus will emit the same amount of CO2 as a high speed rail (HSR) would.

It is important to use models when teaching. It is especially important to use models when teaching earth science because models help students visualize the various processes the earth goes through as well as spatial relationships between the different elements. Since it is impossible for students to get an inside look at our earth, models illustrate the many internal features of Earth much better than straight text or 2-dimensional drawings.

Building models will also appeal to many different types of learners and help to solidify the objectives of the teacher or the lesson. By taking part in hands-on model building, students are working with, and manipulating material and thus deepening their understanding of various concepts.

32. What will MOST LIKELY result from using models in the classroom?

    A. Using models will help students in understanding difficult science concepts.
    B. Models allow students to turn an abstract idea into a concrete one. *
    C. When students create visual models they are creative and inventive.
    D. The teacher is able to check for understanding quickly.

33. Which statement would the author most likely agree with?

    A. Students learn best when they are given information by a teacher.
    B. Students must conform to the way a teacher presents information.
    C. A teacher must use innovative learning approaches that allow students the opportunity to experience concepts. *
    D. Science is the hardest subject for students to learn.

34.

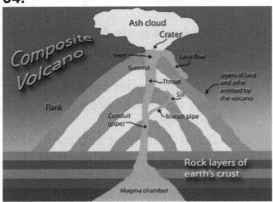

According to the diagram, what happens when a volcano erupts?

A. Lava flows out of the conduit and creates a vent where it then flows out onto the summit.
B. Rock layers are located under the volcano and melt into lave. The lava flows out of the branch pipe and create ashes.
C. Layers of lava and ashes are emitted by the volcano to create the flank.
D. Magma flows up through the conduit and out of the vent of the volcano which is located near the summit. *

35. What is the main idea of the passage?

A. Earth science is difficult to teach without the use of models.
B. Models illustrate ideas in a 3-dimensional way.
C. One way to teach abstract material to students is through the use of models. *
D. Building models appeals to many different types of learners.

36. Which idea best supports why models appeal to many different types of learners?

A. They help students with disabilities understand a difficult topic like earth science.
B. Model building helps students understand spatial relationships.
C. Hands-on learning helps students deepen their understanding of difficult concepts.*
D. When older students build models they are reminded of the good experiences they had in elementary school.

Everyone loves a ripe, juicy tomato. I have found that the best tomatoes are the ones that are home grown. Growing tomatoes may be a <u>daunting</u> task for some, but it doesn't have to be. Many gardeners don't realize that they can germinate tomato seeds indoors about six to eight weeks before the last expected frost of the season. When the danger of frost has passed, a full sun area must be chosen to plant the young seedlings in. Dig holes about the size of a basketball for each plant. Then add a bit of compost and a handful of crushed eggshells for calcium to each of the holes. Make sure each hole is about 12 to 18 inches apart. Mulch around the newly planted seedlings and install supports for the heavy branches.

37. **What do gardeners need to do when they are planting the tomato seedlings?**

   A. Dig holes the size of basketballs and add mulch.
   B. Place the plants 12 to 18 inches apart in large holes that have compost and eggshells.*
   C. Choose a full sun to part shade area for their new plants.
   D. Add some crushed up vitamins that include calcium.

38. **Why might people not want to grow tomatoes at home?**

   A. They might not have had success growing tomato plants from seeds. *
   B. They grow other vegetables in their garden but feel tomatoes are too difficult.
   C. The best tomatoes are the ones that come from the grocery store.
   D. Tomatoes require a lot of tender loving care to grow them successfully.

39. **When the author says that, "Everyone loves a ripe, juicy tomato," in the first sentence, that is a**

   A. Fact
   B. Opinion

40. **From the passage, it can be assumed that**

   A. the author likes the taste of home grown vegetables.*
   B. the author does not enjoy grocery shopping.
   C. the author thinks growing tomatoes is a troublesome task.
   D. the author has grown many vegetable successfully before.

41. **Which is the best synonym for the word <u>daunting?</u>**

   A. tiring
   B. irritating
   C. intimidating*
   D. boring

42. **What is another way the information in the passage could be delivered?**

A. A poster.
B. An insert in a bag of tomatoes.
C. A Venn Diagram
D. Numerical order*

Writing Pre Test

1. A problem is occurring in our nieghborhood that needs immediate attention. **2.** Adolescents rode their skateboards in the middle of the streets and are paying no attention to the cars on the roads. **3.** Although the speed limit within the confines of charter Crossing is 25 miles per hour and drivers need to be aware of pedestrians using the road, a common courtesy needs to be extended to all who use the road. **4.** Therefore, those whom are riding bicycles and skateboards alike must obey the rules of the road that say to stay over to the right hand side of the road. **5.** This especially needs to happen when a car is coming. **6.** It is the responsibility of the skateboarders to move over and allow cars to pass by.

1. **What would be the best way to combine sentences 1 and 2 to make a complete topic sentence?**

   A. A big problem in our neighborhood, adolescents riding skateboards in the middle of the streets.
   B. Adolescents in our neighborhood are riding skateboards in the middle of the street and are not paying attention to the oncoming cars.
   C. It has become a problem that adolescents in our neighborhood are riding their skateboards in the middle of the street and are not paying attention to the oncoming cars.
   D. One problem in our neighborhood is that adolescents are riding their skateboards in the middle of the streets.

2. **Which of these ideas does not help to develop the main idea of the passage?**

   A. The speed limit in Charter Crossing is 25 miles per hour.
   B. Those who ride bicycles or skateboards must obey the rules of the road.
   C. Skateboard riders need to stay over to the right hand side of the road especially when cars are coming.
   D. It is the responsibility of the skateboarders to move over.

3. **Which part of the passage should be corrected to use the correct relative pronoun?**

   A. Part 1: Change "that" to "which"
   B. Part 3: Change "who" to "whom"
   C. Part 4: Change "whom" to "who"
   D. Part 4: Change "that" to "which"

4. **Which verb needs to be changed to make the sentence correct?**

   A. Part 1: occurring
   B. Part 2: rode
   C. Part 3: aware
   D. Part 4: riding

5. **Which word is misspelled?**

   A. Part 1: neighborhood
   B. Part 2: pedestrians
   C. Part 2: using
   D. Part 4: obey

6. **How should sentence 2 be rewritten?**

   A. Adolescents rode their skateboards in the middle of the streets and aren't paying no attention to the cars on the roads.
   B. Adolescents rode their skateboards in the middle of the street and weren't paying no attention to the cars on the roads.
   C. Adolescents are riding their skateboards in the middle of the street and are paying little attention to the cars on the roads.
   D. Adolescents rode their skateboards in the middle of the street and are paying no attention to the cars on the roads.

7. **What needs to be capitalized in the passage?**

   A. Part 1: Neighborhoods
   B. Part 3: Charter
   C. Part 3: Miles Per Hour
   D. Part 6: Skateboarders

Dear Mr. Gonzalez,

1. I recently saw the play *The Sound of Music* that was put on by a local theatre company here in my town. **2**. Being familiar with the movie I enjoyed watching the directors version – it was not very diffrent. **3**. The costume designers did a fine job in designing the costumes. **4**. My favorite character was the Captain.

5. I would like to be considered for the internship position that is being offered at your theatre company this summer. **6**. I am hardworking and, as described above, I am very interested in theatre, and all of the parts that go into producing a play. **7**. I look forward to hearing from you soon. **8**. You will not be disappointed in me as an intern with your theatre company.

8. What would be an effective transition for the author to use between paragraphs 1 and 2?

   A. In addition
   B. On the other hand
   C. Consequently
   D. The reason for my letter is

9. Which part of the passage should be revised to correct an error in the use of prepositions?

   A. Part 1: Change "on" to "in"
   B. Part 3: Change "in" to "on"
   C. Part 5: Change "at" to "in"
   D. Part 8: Change "with" to "at"

10. Which word is misspelled?

   A. Part 2: different
   B. Part 4: character
   C. Part 5: offered
   D. Part 8: disappointed

11. Which word needs a change in capitalization?

   A. Part 1: *of*
   B. Part 4: Captain
   C. Part 6: play
   D. Part 8: company

12. Which part of the passage requires a comma?

   A. Part 2: Being familiar with the movie I enjoyed watching the directors version.
   B. Part 3: The costume designer did a fine job in designing the costumes.
   C. Part 5: I would like to be considered for the internship that is being offered at your theatre company this summer.
   D. Part 8: You will not be disappointed in me as an intern with your theatre company.

13. Which part of the passage requires an apostrophe?

   A. Part 2: directors
   B. Part 3: designers
   C. Part 3: costumes
   D. Part 6: parts

1   A new genre of books that has become very popular amongst children and teens is the graphic novel. 2. Graphic novels have been around for a very long time, first popularized in 1978 with Will Eisner's *A Contract with God,* the genre has become very popular and is even being used for instructional purposes in todays classrooms. 3. Teachers today like to use graphic novels as instructional materials with many of their students.

4. The definition of graphic novels are any book that is formatted like a comic book, but resembles a novel in length and narrative development. 5. They have found their way into classrooms all over because they motivate many reluctant readers to pick up a book. 6. Generaly boys do not tend to be avid readers. 7. However, because of there picture support and high interest content boys in particular are gravitating toward this new genre of book.

14. What would be a better topic sentence for the second paragraph?

   A. Comic books and graphic novels are one and the same.
   B. Boys in particular are interested in reading graphic novels.
   C. Teachers like to use graphic novels as instructional material in their classrooms.
   D. Graphic novels have found their way into many classrooms because they motivate many reluctant readers to read.

15. Which sentence could be deleted from the passage because of redundancy?

   A. Sentence 3
   B. Sentence 4
   C. Sentence 5
   D. Sentence 6

16. Which sentence should have a period instead of a comma?

   A. Sentence 2
   B. Sentence 4
   C. Sentence 6
   D. Sentence 7

17. What is the correct way to revise sentence 4?

   A. The definition graphic novels is any book that is formatted like a comic book, but resembles a novel in length and narrative development.
   B. The definition of graphic novels is any books that is formatted like a comic book, but resembles a novel in length and narrative development.
   C. The definition of graphic novels are any books that are formatted like comic books but resemble novels in length and narrative development.
   D. The definition of a graphic novel is any book that is formatted like a comic book but resembles a novel in length and narrative development.

18. **How should sentence 5 be revised to be clearer?**

   A. The teachers have found their way into classrooms all over because they motivate many reluctant readers to pick up a book.
   B. Graphic novels have found their way into classrooms all over because they motivate many reluctant readers to pick up a book.
   C. Students have found their way into classrooms all over because they motivate many reluctant readers to pick up a book.
   D. Genres have found their way into classrooms all over because they motivate many reluctant readers to pick up a book.

19. **Which sentence contains the wrong form of their/there/they're?**

   A. Sentence 3
   B. Sentence 5
   C. Sentence 6
   D. Sentence 7

20. **Which sentence has a misspelled word in it?**

   A. Sentence 4
   B. Sentence 5
   C. Sentence 6
   D. Sentence 7

21. **Which sentence is missing a comma?**

   A. Sentence 1
   B. Sentence 2
   C. Sentence 5
   D. Sentence 6

22. **Which sentence needs an apostrophe added?**

   A. Sentence 2
   B. Sentence 3
   C. Sentence 4
   D. Sentence 5

1 A very interesting creature that inhabit the sea is the sea horse. **2** Did you realize that sea horses are members of the fish family? **3** They do not have scales like fish but instead have a tough layer of bony plates that are just like a suit of armor. **4** Something else that makes the sea horse interesting is the way their young are birthed. **5** Female sea horses lay eggs – up to 200. **6** But the interesting thing is that they lay their eggs inside a pouch in the male sea horses body. **7** After laying the eggs, the female swims off returning everyday to quickly "check" on her mate.

8 A sea horses curly tail actually has a purpose. **9** Not only beautiful but useful, the sea horse can grasp tightly onto a blade of Sea Grass and anchor the male while he rocks and shakes in order for the pouch to expand to allow the newborn sea horses to be released. **10** It takes about two to six weeks for the babies to begin to move around inside the males pouch. **11** Now he knows it is time for the babies to be born. **12** Sometimes it can take two days for all of the babies to be released from the father's pouch.

23. **What is the topic sentence of the first paragraph?**

   A. A very interesting creature that inhabits the sea is the sea horse.
   B. Did you realize that sea horses are members of the fish family?
   C. Female sea horses lay eggs – up to 200.
   D. The female swims off returning everyday to quickly "check" on her mate.

24. **Which sentence shows some redundancy?**

   A. Sentence 3
   B. Sentence 4
   C. Sentence 9
   D. Sentence 11

25. **How should the sentences in paragraph 2 be reorganized to improve fluency?**

   A. 8, 9, 11, 12, 10
   B. 9, 8, 11, 10, 12
   C. 10, 11, 8, 9, 12
   D. 11, 10, 8, 9, 12

26. **Which sentence has a verb in its incorrect form?**

   A. Sentence 1
   B. Sentence 4
   C. Sentence 5
   D. Sentence 7

27. Which sentence has misplaced or dangling modifiers?

A. Sentence 1
B. Sentence 7
C. Sentence 9
D. Sentence 12

28. Which sentence contains an error in capitalization?

A. Sentence 7
B. Sentence 9
C. Sentence 10
D. Sentence 12

29. Which sentence is missing a comma?

A. Sentence 3
B. Sentence 4
C. Sentence 9
D. Sentence 12

30. Which sentence is the most effective way to transition from paragraph 1 to paragraph 2?

A. The sea horse is an interesting creature.
B. In addition, sea grass is very important to the lives of sea horses.
C. Furthermore, it takes about two to six weeks for the babies to begin moving.
D. Another interesting thing about sea horses is how they are born.

1 Swimming is something that can be fun or competitive. **2** Perhaps you have a fond memory of childhood playing Marco Polo, or just playing in the surf at the beach with your family. **3** Swimming is a sport that can be enjoyed by everyone regardless of one's age. **4** During competition however, swimmers compete in the butterfly, breaststroke, backstroke, and freestyle.

5 Many swimmers say that freestyle is the easiest stroke to swim. **6** Butterfly is thought to be a very difficult stroke to swim. **7** To swim the butterfly swimmers must work at timing their arm pulls to their kicks. **8** In butterfly, swimmers swoop both arms simultaneously over their heads and make an hourglass type motion underneath the water before repeating. **9** At the same time, swimmers must "dolphin kick". **10** A dolphin kick requires swimmers to keep their feet together in order to propel their bodies forward. **11** The kick is termed a dolphin kick because when the feet are kept together, it resembles a dolphin in the water. **12** Perhaps those that think butterfly is difficult is because it requires great strength and endurance from the swimmer.

31. What is the thesis statement for this essay?

- A. Swimming is something that can be fun or competitive.
- B. Swimming is a sport that can be enjoyed by everyone regardless of one's age.
- C. During competition swimmers compete in the butterfly, breaststroke, backstroke, and freestyle.
- D. Butterfly is thought to be a very difficult stroke to swim.

32. Which sentence does not contribute to the development of the main idea of the passage?

- A. Sentence 5
- B. Sentence 6
- C. Sentence 7
- D. Sentence 10

33. Which sentence should come first in the second paragraph?

- A. Sentence 5
- B. Sentence 6
- C. Sentence 7
- D. Sentence 9

34. Which sentence could be deleted from the passage because it is repetitive?

- A. Sentence 6
- B. Sentence 9
- C. Sentence 11
- D. Sentence 12

35. **What would be a good topic sentence for the third paragraph of the essay?**

    A. Breaststroke is another stroke that is swum during competition.
    B. Swimming has become a popular sport in the Olympics.
    C. Swimmers usually specialize in one or two of the four competitive strokes.
    D. An individual medley, or IM, is when the swimmer swims all four strokes in a certain order.

The following sentences contain two errors each (e.g., in construction, grammar, usage, spelling, capitalization, punctuation). Rewrite the text so that the errors are addressed and the original meaning is maintained.

36. **Although the traffic seemed light on routes 295 West and 95 north we decided to take route 301 instead.**

37. **A popular vacation spot to visit for relaxation are sunny beaches in the Caribbean.**

38. **The Henderson's put there dog in the kennel around the corner while they were on vacation.**

39. **The reading passage the students had to read was titled Walking on the Moon and although it was well written it was long.**

40. **We all like when mom drives because she lets us listen to the stations that we want to listen too.**

41. **Which street does you live on?**

42. **A good study skill to develop is to quickly read over the material, than note the major points and finally add in details that support the major points.**

SAMPLE ESSAYS

Essay #1

Use the passage below to prepare a summary of 100-150 words.

In the most publicized views of Response to Intervention (RtI), a pyramid is used to help provide a visual model of the concept. The completed pyramid represents the complete school population. It is typically divided into portions to represent the different instructional levels which one can find in any school across the country.

The largest portion of the pyramid is the bottom section, Tier I. This area represents students who are successful with the regular education curriculum as written. The students in this section are students who are able to meet the standards set forth by the State Departments of Education. Typically, in a school system with a solid curriculum in place, approximately eighty percent of students will fall in this tier.

Students in this tier are successful in their learning with regular delivery of instruction and are in need of almost no additional support to demonstrate their success. Any supports needed are easily delivered within the regular classroom, by regular education teachers.

Support for students in this tier may be necessary, but would fall under the category of simple interventions. Simple interventions are defined as an intervention which can be delivered in the regular classroom by the regular educator using differentiated learning techniques.

The next section of the pyramid is smaller and represents students who may require some additional support or intervention to be able to demonstrate proficiency on assessments. These may include students who are in need of additional repetitions, those considered Title I, English Language Learners, or other learners within the classroom. The model and research indicate that this should be around fifteen percent of the student population.

Students may require supplemental intervention in various formats. Some students may require additional help for a short period of time and be able to return to the regular curriculum and be successful. Another group of students in this tier may require ongoing supplemental intervention for a large portion of their school career in order to maintain adequate progress. This intervention may simply be an extra repetition or may include different materials or groupings.

Supplemental intervention should be goal based. By goal-based, it is important for the supplemental intervention to be specific and meaningful in nature. Having a focus can help to reduce the amount of time it will take a student to acquire the necessary skills to be successful within the regular education curriculum without these supports. Writing goals are often difficult for teachers and requires a thoughtful process, but is crucial to ensuring appropriate instruction is provided. Supplemental intervention involves an increase in the type of interventions provided to the students. This increase from simple interventions to moderate interventions allows more students to achieve success.

The top triangle portion of the pyramid model represents Tier III instruction. This is the most intensive tier of instruction. Students in this tier require significant changes to their curriculum in order to be successful. These students are often several grade levels below their same age peers or may be lacking in significant skills. Often these students may be receiving special education services.

Students in this tier are in need of intensive interventions to ensure progress toward state standards. This is a very small portion of a school population and includes five or less percent.

Essay #2

Read the passages that follow about school vouchers. Then follow the instructions for writing your composition.

School Vouchers are Necessary for Public Education to Succeed

Public education is failing. Students are graduating without the necessary skills to be successful in the job market. School systems require incentive to improve and will not do so without ongoing competition. In order to provide the necessary competition to improve the quality of education students are receiving, voucher systems must be implemented.

School Vouchers will be the End of Public Education

School vouchers will further hurt the public education system by removing critical funding from the schools that desperately need the funds to improve. School systems are not businesses and cannot react immediately to the supply-demand theory in place in many businesses. If employed, the public education system will crumble leaving more students ill prepared for the job market.

Your purpose is to write a composition that will be read by a classroom instructor, in which you will take a position on the issues described in the passages about school vouchers. Be sure to use logical arguments to defend your position and include appropriate examples.

ANSWER KEY

Reading

1. B
2. C
3. D
4. C
5. C
6. C
7. A
8. B
9. A
10. B
11. C
12. D
13. C
14. A
15. B
16. A
17. B
18. D
19. B
20. B
21. B
22. C
23. A
24. A
25. D
26. C
27. A
28. D

29. B
30. C
31. C
32. B
33. C
34. D
35. C
36. C
37. B
38. A
39. B
40. A
41. C
42. D

Writing

1. C
2. A
3. C
4. B
5. A
6. C
7. B
8. D
9. C
10. A
11. B
12. A

13. A
14. D
15. A
16. A
17. D
18. B
19. D
20. C
21. D
22. A
23. A
24. C
25. C
26. A
27. B
28. B
29. A
30. D
31. C
32. A
33. B
34. C
35. A
36. See rationale
37. See rationale
38. See rationale
39. See rationale
40. See rationale
41. See rationale
42. See rationale

RATIONALES

Reading Pre Test Rationales

DIRECTIONS: *Read the passages and answer the questions that follow.*

Marching band music began with organized armies. It was necessary for troops to move in a <u>synchronized</u> fashion. Before musical instruments were introduced, a leader would chant or use drum beats to keep the men organized. Music was added to keep the soldiers in good spirits. During the Revolutionary War, soldiers marched to tunes played by fifes and drums. Later, during the Civil War, soldiers marched to bugle corps and drums. During World War I, soldiers marched to bands that played brass and wood wind instruments as well as the drums. The music played during World War I was more elaborate and more enjoyable to listen to than that of music played during other wars. Marching band music also played an important role in the development of jazz.

1. **What does the word <u>synchronized</u> mean in the passage?**

   A. Robotic
   B. Organized
   C. Musical
   D. Revolutionary

Answer B: The word organized is used in the first sentence of the passage and the sentence following *synchronized. Before musical instruments were introduced, a leader would chant or use drum beats to keep the men organized.*

2. **What is the main idea of the passage?**

   A. The music played changed in different wars.
   B. Soldiers marched to music in order to keep their spirits uplifted.
   C. Marching band music originated with organized armies.
   D. Jazz became important because of marching band music.

Answer C: The main idea is stated in the first sentence. Choice C conveys the same idea using different wording.

3. **What is the author's opinion about marching band music?**

    A. The author likes marching band music.
    B. The author doesn't believe music is a necessary part of war.
    C. The author does not understand the connection between music and war.
    D. The author believes that the music of World War I was the best music.

Answer D: The author states his opinion that the music of World War I was, "more elaborate and more enjoyable to listen to." Therefore, the author is saying that he thinks it is the best.

4. **Why did the author include the last sentence in the passage, "Marching band music also played an important role in the development of jazz"?**

    A. The author is connecting the history of marching band music to the history of jazz.
    B. The author wants to expose the reader to different types of music.
    C. The author wants to connect marching band music, jazz, and past wars to the history of music.
    D. The author believes that all music is connected to the origination of jazz.

Answer A: Choice A is the *best* answer. Choice C might make sense, but the history of music is not mentioned; the history of jazz is though. Choice D is not feasible because the author never makes this statement.

5. **Why did music replace the chanting of early soldiers?**

    A. Music was easier for the soldiers to hear than chanting.
    B. Music kept the soldiers more synchronized with each other.
    C. Music improved the soldier's moods and attitudes.
    D. Music allowed the soldiers to march faster.

Answer C: The passage states that, "Music was added to keep the soldiers in good spirits." This is another way of saying that music improved the soldiers moods and attitudes.

6. Which is a fact presented in this passage?

A. Soldiers preferred the marching band music over the chanting of other soldiers.
B. The music of World War I was more developed than the music heard during other wars.
C. During the Civil War soldiers marched to bugles and drums.
D. Marching band music is the most important aspect of jazz music.

Answer C: A fact is something that cannot be disputed. Choice C is the only choice that cannot be disputed – it is a fact.

7. What type of organizational pattern did the author use in this passage?

A. Classification
B. Compare-and-contrast
C. Cause-and-effect
D. Narrative

Answer A: The author is explaining how marching band music originated and then connects marching band music to the origination of jazz. This is considered classification.

Dance Liners Studio is offering special opportunities to current dance member's families and to new families. If a new dancer is referred to the studio, the family that made the referral will receive $25 off of their October tuition fee. Another incentive that is being offered is a "Change of Studio". If someone has already registered their dancer at another dance <u>locale</u> and paid a non-refundable registration fee, they may register at *Dance Liners* instead and the amount already paid will be deducted from their registration fee. A family must simply show a copy of the check they wrote to the other studio. The next registration date will be August 16 – 20. Your help is greatly appreciated in growing our successful dance program and school.

8. **What is another word that could be substituted for the word _locale_ in the passage?**

    A. class
    B. school
    C. local
    D. avenue

Answer B: Although Choice A would make sense, a word that means the same as *locale* is *school* in this sentence since locale is the place.

9. **What is the main idea of the passage?**

    A. Special incentives are being offered to increase enrollment at *Dance Liners.*
    B. A "Change of Studio" incentive is being offered by *Dance Liners.*
    C. Current families of *Dance Liners* will be offered a $25 reduction in tuition.
    D. The next registration dates are August 16 – 20.

Answer A: Choices B, C, and D are all supporting details of the main idea that special incentives are being offered to increase enrollment at *Dance Liners.*

10. **What is the author's purpose in writing this piece?**

    A. To inform new families of the next registration dates for *Dance Liners Studio.*
    B. To persuade current families to recruit new families to *Dance Liners.*
    C. To inform current families of specials being offered by the studio.
    D. To persuade new families to try a dance class at *Dance Liners Studio.*

Answer B: This is clearly a persuasive piece of writing. Both Choice B and D say the author wrote the piece to persuade, but only Choice B was to persuade families of current dancers.

11. Who is the intended audience for this passage?

    A. Current students of *Dance Liners Studio.*
    B. Those who plan to register for dance classes between August 16 – 20.
    C. Families who are currently enrolled at *Dance Liners* who may know other interested dancers.
    D. Dancers who are already enrolled in another dance studio.

Answer C: Although the first sentence of the passage mentions incentives for both current dance families and new families, the passage is written for current families to try and recruit, or pass along the word, to new dance families.

12. What conclusion can be drawn from this passage?

    A. *Dance Liners Studio* is empathetic to tough economic times and is trying to help families save some money.
    B. *Dance Liners Studio* has added classes to their fall line up.
    C. More dance studios were started and they are all competing for the same business.
    D. Enrollment is down for upcoming classes at *Dance Liners*.

Answer D: Choice D is the correct answer because the reader can decide that if enrollment had increased or the studio was almost to capacity, incentives would not need to be made.

13. What would be the best graphic representation to accompany this passage?

    A. A pictograph that shows the number of dancers in each class.
    B. A line graph that shows enrollment for each year since the studio opened.
    C. A table that shows the classes offered and the times.
    D. A bar graph that shows the various fees for each class.

Answer C: Choices C and D are the only two possible answers. Choice C is a better choice however, because current families can pass the chart along to any new possible families for them to decide if the classes and times will work for their dancer and family schedule.

I believe that history does indeed repeat itself. Currently the post office is looking for ways to be more <u>efficient</u>, and save money in the process. They have raised the prices of stamps continually since 1885. In 1885 the price of a stamp was $ .02. Today, it costs $ .44 to mail a letter and rates are expected to increase again in 2011. Another venue that the postal service is exploring in order to reduce costs is to reduce the number of delivery days from 6 to 5 forgoing Saturday delivery. The problems the postal service is experiencing have, in part, been blamed on the Internet and the increased usage of email, fax machines, and cellular phones.

The problems that the postal service is facing are not new ideas however. The Pony Express, a special mail service that existed in 1860, was much faster than regular mail. In order for a piece of mail to be delivered from Missouri to California, it took the regular mail approximately three weeks. The Pony Express was able to deliver the same letter in 10 days. However, the Pony Express only lasted about 18 months. In 1861 the telegraph was invented and messages could be sent by wire to California much faster than the Pony Express.

I don't think that the United States Postal Service will cease to exist anytime soon. However, history is often a great measure of what is to come in the future.

14. What does the word <u>efficient</u> mean in the first paragraph?

    A. systematic
    B. quick
    C. thrifty
    D. compromising

Answer A: By being systematic, the post office would become more efficient and save money in the process. Systematic and efficient are synonyms.

15. What is the implied main idea of this passage?

    A. The postal service today is better off than the Pony Express of the 1800s.
    B. History can be used as a predictor of what will become of the United States Postal Service.
    C. Technology is the only factor responsible for the decline of the postal service.
    D. The Pony Express was destined to fail based on historical information.

Answer B: Although the author does not state that the postal service will fail, he does imply this idea by linking similar historical events to the problems the postal service is facing today.

16. **Which group of people would MOST LIKELY not respond favorably to this passage?**

   A. Postal workers
   B. History teachers
   C. Information Technology specialists
   D. The US Government

Answer A: Since postal workers would be the group of people most affected by the decline of the postal service, they most likely would not respond well to the information presented in this passage.

17. **What is being compared in this passage?**

   A. The price of stamps
   B. The problems facing the postal service.
   C. Technology of today and yesterday.
   D. The speed of the Pony Express and regular mail.

Answer B: The problems that caused the demise of the Pony Express, which was part of the postal service, are being compared to the problems facing the postal service today.

18. **What argument does the author offer to support the idea that the US Postal Service is declining?**

   A. The price of stamps has increased steadily since 1885.
   B. Increased dependence on technology.
   C. Lack of efficiency and continued economic decline.
   D. Historical information about the postal service in the past.

Answer D: Choices A, B, and C are all problems the postal service must contend with. But, the argument the author offers to support the decline in the postal service is historical references and documentation.

19. **Which would be the best diagram to show the change in price of postage stamps over time?**

   A. A pie chart
   B. A bar graph
   C. A pictograph
   D. A stem and leaf chart

Answer B: A bar graph would allow readers to easily compare the height of the bars to visually see how postage stamp prices have changed over history.

In 1966 Miranda rights were decided upon and put into law. Miranda required all police officers to notify suspects that were taken into custody that they had the right to remain silent and have a lawyer represent them, even if they were unable to afford one. However, the law has now become a little <u>muddled</u>. Although law officials are still required to read suspects their Miranda rights one big change that has taken affect is that suspects must now verbally notify police officials that they would like to <u>invoke</u> their "right to remain silent". In other words, they must break their silence. In addition, suspects must also tell police that they want a lawyer present during their questioning. Unbelievably, if suspects actually "remain silent" in essence what they are doing is waiving their rights to have an attorney present when they truly choose to remain silent. So, although those who are read their Miranda rights are told that they "have the right to remain silent", they truly don't even have this right any more.

20. What does the author use the word *muddled* in the passage to mean?

    A. complicated
    B. unclear
    C. shorter
    D. different

Answer B: Choices A, B, and D would work within the context of the passage. However, the best answer is B unclear. The law has become muddled or unclear compared to the way it was.

21. Which detail supports the idea that the Miranda law has changed?

    A. Suspects must tell police officers that they do not want to say anything.
    B. Suspects must remain silent if they wish to have their Miranda rights upheld.
    C. Officers must read anyone taken into custody their Miranda rights.
    D. It is not necessary to tell police that they want a lawyer – one will be appointed to them automatically.

Answer B: Choices B, C, and D are ideas that support how the law used to be upheld. Choice A describes one of the changes that has gone into effect.

22. Why did the author use the word *unbelievably* in the following sentence from the passage?

"Unbelievably, if suspects actually "remain silent" in essence what they are doing is waiving their rights to have an attorney present..."

A. The author agrees with this change in the law.
B. The author is showing that this idea is not factual.
C. The author thinks the idea stated in the sentence is ridiculous.
D. The author believes that suspects should not be allowed a lawyer.

Answer C: By using the word unbelievably and putting quotation marks around "remain silent", the author is implying that they feel that what suspects must do is the opposite of what the law actually says. They think the idea is ridiculous.

23. What does the word *invoke* mean in the passage?

A. apply
B. pass up
C. be notified
D. pay for

Answer A: By invoking their right to remain silent, suspects are applying or utilizing their right to remain silent.

24. Does the author show any evidence of bias in this passage?

A. Yes
B. No

Answer A: It is quite clear that the author thinks that the changes made to the law were unnecessary and have made the law less clear and more entrapping.

25. What is the BEST summary for the above passage?

    A. Miranda rights have been in effect since 1966.
    B. Miranda requires all police officials to notify suspects of their rights upon being taken into custody.
    C. Suspects have the right to remain silent but only if they alert officials of their desire to do so.
    D. There have been some changes made to the Miranda law since the law was put into place in 1966.

Answer D: Choices A, B, and C are all supporting details about changes that have gone into effect. Choice D is the only idea that applies to the whole passage.

The environment and its future have been a top concern of citizens and politicians around the globe. Environmentalists, engineers, and high-ranking officials have been brainstorming ways to continue to grow economies without harming the environment. China is one country that has proven dedicated to this cause and is developing a three-dimensional fast bus. The concept is so interesting in that the bus will "straddle" cars as it carries passengers above. Therefore, no new roadways need to be built or changed since simple tracks are all that the bus needs to follow and these can be installed along the sides of existing roadways. The new speed bus will run on a combination of electricity and solar power and will be able to move up to 60 kilometers per hour as well as carry between 1,200 and 1,600 people. Chinese engineers are not straddling the fence on this new innovative idea; the first tracks are scheduled to be installed toward the conclusion of 2010.

26. Why does the author say that, "Chinese engineers are not straddling the fence on this new innovative idea…"?

   A. The Chinese are known to move slowly on new and innovative ideas.
   B. There are still logistical ideas to be figured out before the project can move forward.
   C. The author used the figure of speech to show that the Chinese are moving quickly on their new "straddling" bus idea.
   D. The author wants to show that this is not an old fashioned idea by using this figure of speech.

Answer C: Straddling the fence is a figure of speech that usually means someone is having a hard time deciding between several options. Since the Chinese are moving forward quickly with the straddling bus idea, they are doing the opposite and the author chose to play on the word "straddle".

27. How does the author support the idea that the new fast bus is interesting?

   A. The bus will straddle cars as it carries passengers above.
   B. No new roadways need to be built or changed.
   C. The new fast bus follows tracks that run alongside preexisting roadways.
   D. The bus will be able to move up to 60 kilometers per hour.

Answer A: The most interesting idea about the new fast bus is its design. It will straddle cars. Although the other choices are supporting details that describe the bus further, they do not support the opinion that it is interesting.

28. Who would MOST LIKELY be the most interested in reading this article?

   A. Chinese government officials.
   B. United States engineers.
   C. Anyone traveling to China toward the end of 2010.
   D. Environmentally conscious citizens.

Answer D: Although many people would be interested in reading about this new innovative idea, since the fast bus was designed with environmental concerns in mind, environmentally conscious citizens would be most interested in this article so that they can learn about a large project that is beginning to help preserve the environment.

29. What conclusion can be drawn about the Chinese from this passage?

   A. The Chinese are a very competitive nation.
   B. The Chinese can be classified as an innovative nation.
   C. The fast bus project will be completed very quickly.
   D. No one is interested in riding the fast bus over driving their cars.

Answer B: The best answer is B. The Chinese are the first nation to design and construct an alternative form of transportation that can be easily integrated into the infrastructure of Beijing and will also preserve the environment. This is very innovative.

30. The author states that the environment has been a top concern to those around the globe. Which idea BEST supports this idea?

   A. Chinese engineers are not straddling the fence on implementing the fast bus.
   B. Environmentalists, engineers and high-ranking officials have been brainstorming ways to continue to grow economies while preserving the environment.
   C. China is developing the fast bus and will begin production as early as 2010.
   D. The new speed bus will run on a combination of electricity and solar power.

Answer C: Because preserving the environment has been a top concern, China is moving forward quickly on an alternative form of transportation for the residents and visitors to Beijing.

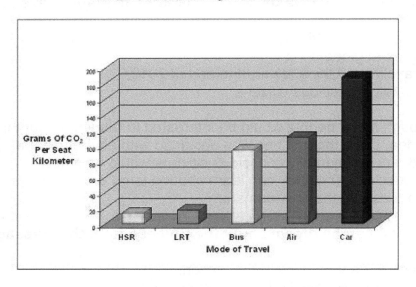

CO$_2$ Generated By Travel Mode

Grams Of CO$_2$ Per Seat Kilometer

Mode of Travel

HSR   LRT   Bus   Air   Car

31. Which conclusion can be drawn from the graph above?

A. The new fast bus will emit the same amount of CO2 as a car.
B. It is better to fly than to take a bus to a location in order to reduce the amount of CO2 being emitted into the air.
C. The new fast bus will reduce the amount of CO2 emissions.
D. The fast bus will emit the same amount of CO2 as a high speed rail (HSR) would.

Answer C: The bar graph shows that cars emit the most CO2. Therefore, the fast bus will surely emit less CO2 than the cars currently do.

It is important to use models when teaching. It is especially important to use models when teaching earth science because models help students visualize the various processes the earth goes through as well as spatial relationships between the different elements. Since it is impossible for students to get an inside look at our earth, models illustrate the many internal features of Earth much better than straight text or 2-dimensional drawings.

Building models will also appeal to many different types of learners and help to solidify the objectives of the teacher or the lesson. By taking part in hands-on model building, students are working with, and manipulating material and thus deepening their understanding of various concepts.

32. What will MOST LIKELY result from using models in the classroom?

    A. Using models will help students in understanding difficult science concepts.
    B. Models allow students to turn an abstract idea into a concrete one.
    C. When students create visual models they are creative and inventive.
    D. The teacher is able to check for understanding quickly.

Answer B: Although Choice A is a possible result of using models, it specifically states students will understand only difficult science concepts. Choice B is broad enough to state that students will be able to better understand abstract concepts in any discipline by making them into concrete ideas through the use of models.

33. Which statement would the author most likely agree with?

    A. Students learn best when they are given information by a teacher.
    B. Students must conform to the way a teacher presents information.
    C. A teacher must use innovative learning approaches that allow students the opportunity to experience concepts.
    D. Science is the hardest subject for students to learn.

Answer C: It is clear that the author supports the use of models to promote understanding in the classroom. Choice C is the only choice that matches this idea.

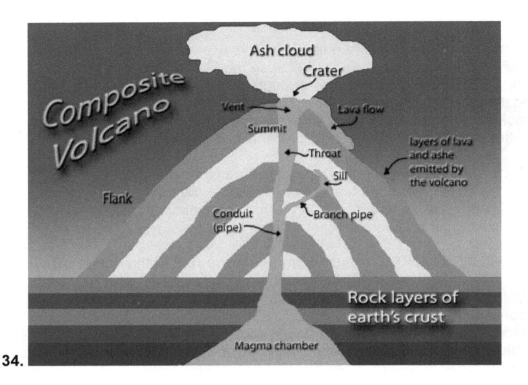

34.

According to the diagram, what happens when a volcano erupts?

    A. Lava flows out of the conduit and creates a vent where it then flows out onto the summit.

    B. Rock layers are located under the volcano and melt into lave. The lava flows out of the branch pipe and create ashe.

    C. Layers of lava and ashe are emitted by the volcano to create the flank.

    D. Magma flows up through the conduit and out of the vent of the volcano which is located near the summit.

Answer D: In order to answer this question correctly, the terms used in each choice must be checked against the diagram. In Choice D, the correct term of magma is used instead of lava. Magma becomes lava once it flows outside of the volcano. While inside, it is called magma.

35. What is the main idea of the passage?

   A. Earth science is difficult to teach without the use of models.
   B. Models illustrate ideas in a 3-dimensional way.
   C. One way to teach abstract material to students is through the use of models.
   D. Building models appeals to many different types of learners.

Answer C: Choices A, B, and D are all supporting details of the main idea, Choice C.

36. Which idea best supports why models appeal to many different types of learners?

   A. They help students with disabilities understand a difficult topic like earth science.
   B. Model building helps students understand spatial relationships.
   C. Hands-on learning helps students deepen their understanding of difficult concepts.
   D. When older students build models they are reminded of the good experiences they had in elementary school.

Answer C: Although other choices may be good choices, Choice C is the only one that is actually mentioned in the passage as a supporting detail.

Everyone loves a ripe, juicy tomato. I have found that the best tomatoes are the ones that are home grown. Growing tomatoes may be a daunting task for some, but it doesn't have to be. Many gardeners don't realize that they can germinate tomato seeds indoors about six to eight weeks before the last expected frost of the season. When the danger of frost has passed, a full sun area must be chosen to plant the young seedlings in. Dig holes about the size of a basketball for each plant. Then add a bit of compost and a handful of crushed eggshells for calcium to each of the holes. Make sure each hole is about 12 to 18 inches apart. Mulch around the newly planted seedlings and install supports for the heavy branches.

37. What do gardeners need to do when they are planting the tomato seedlings?

  A. Dig holes the size of basketballs and add mulch.
  B. Place the plants 12 to 18 inches apart in large holes that have compost and eggshells.*
  C. Choose a full sun to part shade area for their new plants.
  D. Add some crushed up vitamins that include calcium.

Answer B: Readers must go back into the passage to revisit the step in planting new tomatoes. Readers must also focus on the details of each step. In Choice A the holes need to be the size of basketballs but mulch does not need to be added to the hole. Choice C says full sun to part shade; tomatoes need full sun. Finally, crushed eggshells need to be added for calcium, not vitamins. Therefore, the best answer is B.

38. Why might people not want to grow tomatoes at home?

  A. They might not have had success growing tomato plants from seeds.
  B. They grow other vegetables in their garden but feel tomatoes are too difficult.
  C. The best tomatoes are the ones that come from the grocery store.
  D. Tomatoes require a lot of tender loving care to grow them successfully.

Answer A: Since the passage focuses on growing tomatoes from seedlings the best choice is A.

39. When the author says that, "Everyone loves a ripe, juicy tomato," in the first sentence, that is a(n)

A. Fact
B. Opinion

Answer B: Since the word "everyone" is used the sentence is an opinion. Everyone might not love ripe juicy tomatoes. Therefore, it is an opinion since it can be argued.

40. From the passage, it can be assumed that

A. the author likes the taste of home grown vegetables.
B. the author does not enjoy grocery shopping.
C. the author thinks growing tomatoes is a troublesome task.
D. the author has grown many vegetable successfully before.

Answer A: The author clearly states in the second sentence, "I have found that the best tomatoes are the ones that are home grown." Therefore, we can assume that the author likes the taste of home grown vegetables.

41. Which is the best synonym for the word <u>daunting?</u>

A. tiring
B. irritating
C. intimidating
D. boring

Answer C: The word that can best be substituted into the passage is intimidating. Many people may not want to grow tomatoes because they are unsure of what to do and may believe that it is harder than it actually is.

42. What is another way the information in the passage could be presented?

A. A poster.
B. An insert in a bag of tomatoes.
C. A Venn Diagram
D. Numerical order

Answer D: Because the steps in growing tomatoes easily are presented in sequential order, another method of presentation would have been to number the steps that should be followed to grow tomatoes.

Writing Pre Test Rationales

DIRECTIONS: *Read the following passages and answer the questions that follow each one.*

1. A problem is occurring in our nieghborhood that needs immediate attention. **2.** Adolescents rode their skateboards in the middle of the streets and are paying no attention to the cars on the roads. **3.** Although the speed limit within the confines of charter Crossing is 25 miles per hour and drivers need to be aware of pedestrians using the road, a common courtesy needs to be extended to all who use the road. **4.** Therefore, those whom are riding bicycles and skateboards alike must obey the rules of the road that say to stay over to the right hand side of the road. **5.** This especially needs to happen when a car is coming. **6.** It is the responsibility of the skateboarders to move over and allow cars to pass by.

1. **What would be the best way to combine sentences 1 and 2 to make a complete topic sentence?**

   A. A big problem in our neighborhood, adolescents riding skateboards in the middle of the streets.
   B. Adolescents in our neighborhood are riding skateboards in the middle of the street and are not paying attention to the oncoming cars.
   C. It has become a problem that adolescents in our neighborhood are riding their skateboards in the middle of the street and are not paying attention to the oncoming cars.
   D. One problem in our neighborhood is that adolescents are riding their skateboards in the middle of the streets.

Answer C: Choice A is an incomplete sentence. Choice B is a well written sentence but does not state that the adolescents in the street are a problem which is the main idea of the passage. Choice D does not state why the adolescents in the streets are a problem which again does not address the main idea of the passage.

2. **Which of these ideas does not help to develop the main idea of the passage?**

   A. The speed limit in Charter Crossing is 25 miles per hour.
   B. Those who ride bicycles or skateboards must obey the rules of the road.
   C. Skateboard riders need to stay over to the right hand side of the road especially when cars are coming.
   D. It is the responsibility of the skateboarders to move over.

Answer A: The problem is not that the adolescents are riding too fast; it is that they are not paying attention to oncoming traffic. The idea of the speed limit applies to the cars.

3. Which part of the passage should be corrected to use the correct relative pronoun?

   A. Part 1: Change "that" to "which"
   B. Part 3: Change "who" to "whom"
   C. Part 4: Change "whom" to "who"
   D. Part 4: Change "that" to "which"

Answer C: Whom is used when it is used as a noun. For example, Whom will you see the movie with?

4. Which verb needs to be changed to make the sentence correct?

   A. Part 1: occurring
   B. Part 2: rode
   C. Part 3: aware
   D. Part 4: riding

Answer B: The word *rode* is the incorrect form of the verb needed in the sentence. The correct form of the verb should be *are riding.*

5. Which word is misspelled?

   A. Part 1: neighborhood
   B. Part 2: pedestrians
   C. Part 2: using
   D. Part 4: obey

Answer A: The rule, "I before e except after c, except for in words like neighbor and weigh" applies here.

6. **How should sentence 2 be rewritten?**

   A. Adolescents rode their skateboards in the middle of the streets and aren't paying no attention to the cars on the roads.
   B. Adolescents rode their skateboards in the middle of the street and weren't paying no attention to the cars on the roads.
   C. Adolescents are riding their skateboards in the middle of the street and are paying little attention to the cars on the roads.
   D. Adolescents rode their skateboards in the middle of the street and are paying no attention to the cars on the roads.

Answer C: The verb forms must agree in *are riding* and *are paying.* "No attention" in the sentence needs to be changed to either *little attention* or *aren't paying attention.*

7. **What needs to be capitalized in the passage?**

   A. Part 1: Neighborhoods
   B. Part 3: Charter
   C. Part 3: Miles Per Hour
   D. Part 6: Skateboarders

Answer B: The word Charter must be capitalized because Charter Crossing is the proper name of the neighborhood.

Dear Mr. Gonzalez,

1. I recently saw the play *The Sound of Music* that was put on by a local theatre company here in my town. **2.** Being familiar with the movie I enjoyed watching the directors version – it was not very diffrent. **3.** The costume designers did a fine job in designing the costumes. **4.** My favorite character was the Captain.

5. I would like to be considered for the internship position that is being offered at your theatre company this summer. **6.** I am hardworking and, as described above, I am very interested in theatre, and all of the parts that go into producing a play. **7.** I look forward to hearing from you soon. **8.** You will not be disappointed in me as an intern with your theatre company.

8. What would be an effective transition for the author to use between paragraphs 1 and 2?

    A. In addition
    B. On the other hand
    C. Consequently
    D. The reason for my letter is

Answer D: Although Choice C may work in this particular case, the best transition is Choice D because it is always a good idea to state the reason you are writing.

9. Which part of the passage should be revised to correct an error in the use of prepositions?

    A. Part 1: Change "on" to "in"
    B. Part 3: Change "in" to "on"
    C. Part 5: Change "at" to "in"
    D. Part 8: Change "with" to "at"

Answer C: The theatre company is a group of people rather than an entity all its own. Therefore, the correct preposition to use is *in.*

10. Which word is misspelled?

    A. Part 2: different
    B. Part 4: character
    C. Part 5: offered
    D. Part 8: disappointed

Answer A: Although the word may be pronounced *different,* the correct spelling is *different.*

11. Which word needs a change in capitalization?

    A. Part 1: *of*
    B. Part 4: Captain
    C. Part 6: play
    D. Part 8: company

Answer B: The captain refers to a person. Had it been used as a proper noun, it would require a capital C.

12. Which part of the passage requires a comma?

    A. Part 2: Being familiar with the movie I enjoyed watching the directors version.
    B. Part 3: The costume designer did a fine job in designing the costumes.
    C. Part 5: I would like to be considered for the internship that is being offered at your theatre company this summer.
    D. Part 8: You will not be disappointed in me as an intern with your theatre company.

Answer A: There is an introductory phrase, *Being familiar with the movie,* and after this phrase a comma is required. *I enjoyed watching the director's version* is a sentence that could stand on its own. Therefore, requiring a comma to come after a phrase that is placed in front of it

13. Which part of the passage requires an apostrophe?

    A. Part 2: directors
    B. Part 3: designers
    C. Part 3: costumes
    D. Part 6: parts

Answer A: In the passage, the version belongs to the director – it is his version of the story. Therefore, an apostrophe is required to show possession.

1 A new genre of books that has become very popular amongst children and teens is the graphic novel. **2.** Graphic novels have been around for a very long time, first popularized in 1978 with Will Eisner's *A Contract with God,* the genre has become very popular and is even being used for instructional purposes in todays classrooms. **3.** Teachers today like to use graphic novels as instructional materials with many of their students.

4. The definition of graphic novels are any book that is formatted like a comic book, but resembles a novel in length and narrative development. **5.** They have found their way into classrooms all over because they motivate many reluctant readers to pick up a book. **6.** Generaly boys do not tend to be avid readers. **7.** However, because of there picture support and high interest content boys in particular are gravitating toward this new genre of book.

14. What would be a better topic sentence for the second paragraph?

    A. Comic books and graphic novels are one and the same.
    B. Boys in particular are interested in reading graphic novels.
    C. Teachers like to use graphic novels as instructional material in their classrooms.
    D. Graphic novels have found their way into many classrooms because they motivate many reluctant readers to read.

Answer D: The second paragraph is about how graphic novels have made their way into the classroom to be used for instructional purposes. Therefore, the topic sentence should reflect this focus.

15. Which sentence could be deleted from the passage because of redundancy?

    A. Sentence 3
    B. Sentence 4
    C. Sentence 5
    D. Sentence 6

Answer A: Sentence 3 basically repeats what sentence 2 stated; that graphic novels are being used for instructional purposes.

16. **Which sentence should have a period instead of a comma?**

    A. Sentence 2
    B. Sentence 4
    C. Sentence 6
    D. Sentence 7

Answer A: There should be a period after the word *time* in sentence 2. If a transition word had been used to start sentence 2, such as *although,* then a comma would be the appropriate punctuation to use.

17. **What is the correct way to revise sentence 4?**

    A. The definition graphic novels is any book that is formatted like a comic book, but resembles a novel in length and narrative development.
    B. The definition of graphic novels is any books that is formatted like a comic book, but resembles a novel in length and narrative development.
    C. The definition of graphic novels are any books that are formatted like comic books but resemble novels in length and narrative development.
    D. The definition of a graphic novel is any book that is formatted like a comic book but resembles a novel in length and narrative development.

Answer D: The verbs *is* and *are* need to agree with the subject. Choice D is the only one that has correct agreement.

18. **How should sentence 5 be revised to be clearer?**

    A. The teachers have found their way into classrooms all over because they motivate many reluctant readers to pick up a book.
    B. Graphic novels have found their way into classrooms all over because they motivate many reluctant readers to pick up a book.
    C. Students have found their way into classrooms all over because they motivate many reluctant readers to pick up a book.
    D. Genres have found their way into classrooms all over because they motivate many reluctant readers to pick up a book.

Answer B: The reason that sentence 5 needs to be revised is because the pronoun *they* is not clearly defined – it is unclear who *they* refers to. Choice B defines *they* as the graphic novels.

19.Which sentence contains the wrong form of their/there/they're?

    A. Sentence 3
    B. Sentence 5
    C. Sentence 6
    D. Sentence 7

Answer D: The correct form needed is *their* because the picture support belongs to the graphic novels – there is possession in this sentence.

20.Which sentence has a misspelled word in it?

    A. Sentence 4
    B. Sentence 5
    C. Sentence 6
    D. Sentence 7

Answer C: When adding a suffix like –ly to a word that ends in *l* already, the *l* is doubled.

21.Which sentence is missing a comma?

    A. Sentence 1
    B. Sentence 2
    C. Sentence 5
    D. Sentence 6

Answer D: After an introductory word, in this case after the word *generally*, a comma is required.

22.Which sentence needs an apostrophe added?

    A. Sentence 2
    B. Sentence 3
    C. Sentence 4
    D. Sentence 5

Answer A: The word *today's* requires an apostrophe because it shows possession.

1 A very interesting creature that inhabit the sea is the sea horse. **2** Did you realize that sea horses are members of the fish family? **3** They do not have scales like fish but instead have a tough layer of bony plates that are just like a suit of armor. **4** Something else that makes the sea horse interesting is the way their young are birthed. **5** Female sea horses lay eggs – up to 200.
6 But the interesting thing is that they lay their eggs inside a pouch in the male sea horses body. **7** After laying the eggs, the female swims off returning everyday to quickly "check" on her mate.

8 A sea horses curly tail actually has a purpose. **9** Not only beautiful but useful, the sea horse can grasp tightly onto a blade of Sea Grass and anchor the male while he rocks and shakes in order for the pouch to expand to allow the newborn sea horses to be released. **10** It takes about two to six weeks for the babies to begin to move around inside the males pouch. **11** Now he knows it is time for the babies to be born. **12** Sometimes it can take two days for all of the babies to be released from the father's pouch.

23. **What is the topic sentence of the first paragraph?**

    A. A very interesting creature that inhabits the sea is the sea horse.
    B. Did you realize that sea horses are members of the fish family?
    C. Female sea horses lay eggs – up to 200.
    D. The female swims off returning everyday to quickly "check" on her mate.

Answer A: The topic sentence of a paragraph is normally the first sentence, but not always. In this case, the first sentence is the topic sentence because it sets the tone for the rest of the paragraph's focus.

24. **Which sentence shows some redundancy?**

    A. Sentence 3
    B. Sentence 4
    C. Sentence 9
    D. Sentence 11

Answer C: Both sentences 8 and 9 state that the sea horses tail has a purpose.

25. How should the sentences in paragraph 2 be reorganized to improve fluency?

   A. 8, 9, 11, 12, 10
   B. 9, 8, 11, 10, 12
   C. 10, 11, 8, 9, 12
   D. 11, 10, 8, 9, 12

Answer C: The correct sequence of events is that the female swims off, the babies begin to move in the male's pouch, he recognizes that it's time for the babies to be born, the male attaches himself to a blade of grass using his tail, and sometimes it can take up to two days for all the babies to be released.

26. Which sentence has a verb in its incorrect form?

   A. Sentence 1
   B. Sentence 4
   C. Sentence 5
   D. Sentence 7

Answer A: The correct form of the verb is inhabits.

27. Which sentence has misplaced or dangling modifiers?

   A. Sentence 1
   B. Sentence 7
   C. Sentence 9
   D. Sentence 12

Answer B: The introductory phrase *"Not only beautiful but useful"* is not explained in the sentence that follows it. It is actually referring to its tail. The sentence should read something like, *"Not only beautiful but also useful, the sea horse's tail…"*

28. Which sentence contains an error in capitalization?

   A. Sentence 7
   B. Sentence 9
   C. Sentence 10
   D. Sentence 12

Answer B: Sea grass is not a proper noun. Therefore, it does not require any capitalization.

29. Which sentence is missing a comma?

A. Sentence 3
B. Sentence 4
C. Sentence 9
D. Sentence 12

Answer A: There should be a comma after the word *fish*, because of the transition word instead.

30. Which sentence is the most effective way to transition from paragraph 1 to paragraph 2?

A. The sea horse is an interesting creature.
B. In addition, sea grass is very important to the lives of sea horses.
C. Furthermore, it takes about two to six weeks for the babies to begin moving.
D. Another interesting thing about sea horses is how they are born.

Answer D: This is the best way to transition between paragraph 1 and paragraph 2 because the whole passage is about how interesting sea horses are. This transition keeps that focus into the next paragraph.

1 Swimming is something that can be fun or competitive. **2** Perhaps you have a fond memory of childhood playing Marco Polo, or just playing in the surf at the beach with your family. **3** Swimming is a sport that can be enjoyed by everyone regardless of one's age. **4** During competition however, swimmers compete in the butterfly, breaststroke, backstroke, and freestyle.

5 Many swimmers say that freestyle is the easiest stroke to swim. **6** Butterfly is thought to be a very difficult stroke to swim. **7** To swim the butterfly swimmers must work at timing their arm pulls to their kicks. **8** In butterfly, swimmers swoop both arms simultaneously over their heads and make an hourglass type motion underneath the water before repeating. **9** At the same time, swimmers must "dolphin kick". **10** A dolphin kick requires swimmers to keep their feet together in order to propel their bodies forward. **11** The kick is termed a dolphin kick because when the feet are kept together, it resembles a dolphin in the water. **12** Perhaps those that think butterfly is difficult is because it requires great strength and endurance from the swimmer.

31. What is the thesis statement for this essay?

A. Swimming is something that can be fun or competitive.
B. Swimming is a sport that can be enjoyed by everyone regardless of one's age.
C. During competition swimmers compete in the butterfly, breaststroke, backstroke, and freestyle.
D. Butterfly is thought to be a very difficult stroke to swim.

Answer C: A thesis statement is the main idea of a passage. It usually appears at the end of the first paragraph and alerts the reader as to what they will read in the following paragraphs.

32. Which sentence does not contribute to the development of the main idea of the passage?

A. Sentence 5
B. Sentence 6
C. Sentence 7
D. Sentence 10

Answer A: The passage is not about which strokes are the easiest or the most difficult to swim. Therefore, sentence 5 is not on topic and detracts from developing the main idea of strokes that are swum during competition.

33. Which sentence should come first in the second paragraph?

    A. Sentence 5
    B. Sentence 6
    C. Sentence 7
    D. Sentence 9

Answer B: As noted in Question 32, Sentence 5 detracts from the main idea of the passage and should therefore not begin the second paragraph.

34. Which sentence could be deleted from the passage because it is repetitive?

    A. Sentence 6
    B. Sentence 9
    C. Sentence 11
    D. Sentence 12

Answer C: Both sentences 10 and 11 are about what a dolphin kick is. Sentence 11 is redundant and therefore, could be deleted from the passage without taking meaning away from the passage.

35. What would be a good topic sentence for the third paragraph of the essay?

    A. Breaststroke is another stroke that is swum during competition.
    B. Swimming has become a popular sport in the Olympics.
    C. Swimmers usually specialize in one or two of the four competitive strokes.
    D. An individual medley, or IM, is when the swimmer swims all four strokes in a certain order.

Answer A: Since the thesis statement of the passage says, "*During competition however, swimmers compete in the butterfly, breaststroke, backstroke, an freestyle*", it would make sense to make the third paragraph about the breaststroke.

The following sentences contain two errors each (e.g., in construction, grammar, usage, spelling, capitalization, punctuation). Rewrite the text so that the errors are addressed and the original meaning is maintained.

36. Although the traffic seemed light on routes 295 West and 95 north we decided to take route 301 instead.

The word *north* needs a capital and there should be a comma following the word *north* since, *"we decided to take route 301 instead"*, could stand alone. The new sentence should read:

Although the traffic seemed light on routes 295 West and 95 North, we decided to take route 301 instead.

37. A popular vacation spot to visit for relaxation are sunny beaches in the Caribbean.

The sentence is awkward and needs to be rearranged. Also, the verb *are* does not agree with the singular *vacation spot.* The new sentence should read:

A popular spot to visit and relax is a sunny beach in the Caribbean.

38. The Henderson's put there dog in the kennel around the corner while they were on vacation.

Hendersons in this sentence is simply a plural word and does not require an apostrophe. The dog does belong to them however, and the correct form of "there" is *their.* The new sentence should read:

The Henderson put their dog in the kennel around the corner while they were on vacation.

39. The reading passage the students had to read was titled Walking on the Moon and although it was well written it was long.

Titles of books must be italicized when typed. When they are handwritten, titles must be underlined. This sentence also requires a comma after the word *written* because "*it was long*" could stand as its own sentence. The new sentence should read:

The reading passage the students had to read was titled Walking on the Moon *and although it was well written, it was long.*

*Note: In the above sentence, the title of the book is not italicized because it would not stand out. When typing in italicized font, titles should be normal; when typing in normal font, titles should be italicized.

40. We all like when mom drives because she lets us listen to the stations that we want to listen too.

Mom is used as a proper noun in this sentence and must be capitalized. The word *too* means also or extreme and is used incorrectly in this sentence. The new sentence should read:

We all like when Mom drives because she lets us listen to the stations that we want to listen to.

41. Which street does you live on?

The preposition *on* needs to be moved to the front of the sentence because it is improper to end a sentence with a preposition. The verb *does* is not the correct form for the word street. The new sentence should read:

On which street do you live?

42. A good study skill to develop is to quickly read over the material, than note the major points and finally add in details that support the major points.

The word *than* should be then. *Than* compares, *then* indicates sequence. This sentence also requires a comma after the word *points* because the sentence has three items in a series and commas come before *and* in this case. The new sentence should read:

A good study skill to develop is to quickly read over the material, then note the major points, and finally add in details that support the major points.

Essay #1

Use the passage below to prepare a summary of 100-150 words.

In the most publicized views of Response to Intervention (RtI), a pyramid is used to help provide a visual model of the concept. The completed pyramid represents the complete school population. It is typically divided into portions to represent the different instructional levels which one can find in any school across the country.

The largest portion of the pyramid is the bottom section, Tier I. This area represents students who are successful with the regular education curriculum as written. The students in this section are students who are able to meet the standards set forth by the State Departments of Education. Typically, in a school system with a solid curriculum in place, approximately eighty percent of students will fall in this tier.

Students in this tier are successful in their learning with regular delivery of instruction and are in need of almost no additional support to demonstrate their success. Any supports needed are easily delivered within the regular classroom, by regular education teachers.

Support for students in this tier may be necessary, but would fall under the category of simple interventions. Simple interventions are defined as an intervention which can be delivered in the regular classroom by the regular educator using differentiated learning techniques.

The next section of the pyramid is smaller and represents students who may require some additional support or intervention to be able to demonstrate proficiency on assessments. These may include students who are in need of additional repetitions, those considered Title I, English Language Learners, or other learners within the classroom. The model and research indicate that this should be around fifteen percent of the student population.

Students may require supplemental intervention in various formats. Some students may require additional help for a short period of time and be able to return to the regular curriculum and be successful. Another group of students in this tier may require ongoing supplemental intervention for a large portion of their school career in order to maintain adequate progress. This intervention may simply be an extra repetition or may include different materials or groupings.

Supplemental intervention should be goal based. By goal-based, it is important for the supplemental intervention to be specific and meaningful in nature. Having a focus can help to reduce the amount of time it will take a student to acquire the necessary skills to be successful within the regular education curriculum without these supports. Writing goals are often difficult for teachers and requires a thoughtful process, but is crucial to ensuring appropriate instruction is provided. Supplemental intervention involves an increase in the type of interventions provided to the students. This increase from simple interventions to moderate interventions allows more students to achieve success.

The top triangle portion of the pyramid model represents Tier III instruction. This is the most intensive tier of instruction. Students in this tier require significant changes to their curriculum in order to be successful. These students are often several grade levels below their same age peers or may be lacking in significant skills. Often these students may be receiving special education services.

Students in this tier are in need of intensive interventions to ensure progress toward state standards. This is a very small portion of a school population and includes five or less percent.

Sample Well-Done Response:

Response to Intervention (RtI) is a model of representing all of a school's population based on its success with achieving the standards and curriculum goals the school system has put into place. It is most often represented using a pyramid to show that each new tier contains fewer students than the previous tiers. There are typically three tiers. The biggest tier, tier one, contains about 80% of the students and contains those students who are successful with the standards and regular curriculum. Tier two contains about 15% of the students and is those students who may need a little extra assistance to meet the standards and curriculum. The final tier, tier three consists of the remaining 5% of the students who are significantly struggling with meeting the needs of the regular curriculum.

Sample Poor Response:

Response to intervention is a method of separating the students into different groups to help them learn the material in schools. There are three groups and the groups are based on what the students know in regards to the curriculum. Each group of students receives the same amount of support and intervention. The third tier is the same as special education. Students who speak a language other than English automatically are in the second tier. Overall, the students in the second and third tiers are those students who are getting poor grades.

Essay #2

Read the passages that follow about school vouchers. Then follow the instructions for writing your composition.

School Vouchers are Necessary for Public Education to Succeed

Public education is failing. Students are graduating without the necessary skills to be successful in the job market. School systems require incentive to improve and will not do so without ongoing competition. In order to provide the necessary competition to improve the quality of education students are receiving, voucher systems must be implemented.

School Vouchers will be the End of Public Education

School vouchers will further hurt the public education system by removing critical funding from the schools that desperately need the funds to improve. School systems are not businesses and cannot react immediately to the supply-demand theory in place in many businesses. If employed, the public education system will crumble leaving more students ill prepared for the job market.

Your purpose is to write a composition that will be read by a classroom instructor, in which you will take a position on the issues described in the passages about school vouchers. Be sure to use logical arguments to defend your position and include appropriate examples.

Sample Well-Done Response:

When reading the papers, listening to the media, or observing new graduates it becomes obvious that school systems are no longer successful. Students lag behind other countries in both reading and math. It is obvious that something needs to be changed. School voucher systems offer students the opportunity to overcome these issues. Voucher systems should be implemented because they ensure that bad schools are eliminated, inefficiency is reduced and social classes are more balanced.

By implementing a voucher system, schools that are no longer effective can be closed, which leaves more funding for schools that are solid. This provides all students with only the best opportunity to obtain the education they deserve. The market forces put into play with the voucher system increase the services and education provided to the students.

Additionally, as schools compete, the inefficiencies must be eliminated or will doom an institution to failure. No longer will inefficient bureaucracies be able to maintain themselves. Students will be attracted to schools that provide the most services at the least possible cost. Students will want to jump through the fewest amounts of hoops possible to ensure their success, and those will be the schools that succeed. Bureaucracies will fail under this model.

Moreover, the implementation of vouchers provides the best opportunity to reduce the social class issues which impede students from lower classes. Children of all economic levels have the opportunity to attend the best school. Regardless of home environment, students have the opportunity to attend the best prepared schools.

It is through the implementation of the school voucher system that our educational system has the best chance to improve. By eliminating poor achieving schools, increasing efficiency and balancing the inequities the social classes face, the United States system the best in the world.

Sample Poor Response:

School voucher systems are necessary to improve the education system. Without school vouchers, schools will not improve. It is only through the use of school vouchers that things can get better. Schools need to get better in order help the students. It is the job of the school system to help students. When schools help students, students learn more. Without vouchers, students won't learn as much. Since schools are about learning it is essential that schools use vouchers.

Vouchers are able to let students choose their schools. Choice is a great part of learning. Students like to make their own choices. Schools will be more popular when students get to choose where they will go. This is another reason vouchers are important.

Finally, vouchers are easy to put in place. They don't cost anyone money, so everyone will be happy. When people don't have to spend money they will use the schools more. This will mean that everyone will learn more. Schools are free and that is important to keep in place. Vouchers let this happen.